ACKNOWLEDGMENTS

We would like to thank the consulting staff at Convergent Computing (CCO) and our clients that contribute to the shared knowledge and expertise that makes the content of these books possible!

Maximizing Microsoft's Azure for Dev, Test, and DevOps Scenarios
Mini-Book Technology Series – Book 3

Authors: Rand Morimoto, Ph.D., MCSE
&
Guy Yardeni, MCITP, CISSP, MVP

DEDICATION

I dedicate this book to my kids Kelly, Noble, Chip,
and Eduardo - Rand Morimoto

I dedicate this book to Zoe and Maya - Guy Yardeni

TABLE OF CONTENTS

INTRODUCTION

Microsoft's Azure is a service offering that many developers have a hard time understanding what all it provides and how they and their development teams can leverage the cloud service. This lack of understanding is Microsoft's own doing as Azure does so many things, it's hard to sit through any "briefing" on Azure and truly understand how all of the pieces fit together to provide an end to end solution. That's because Azure is a development platform, an application hosting platform, a virtual machine hosting platform, a management platform, a monitoring platform, a cloud storage platform, a data analytics platform, among several other things, it just does a LOT of stuff.

Rather than trying to define ALL that Microsoft Azure does, this book focuses specifically on a core area of "Azure as it relates to Dev, Test, and DevOps scenarios." For everything that a typical engineering organization would do to spin up Dev and Test machines, run a variety of operating systems like Linux or Windows, manage the environment with common tools like Puppet, Chef, or Team Foundation Server, image systems, clone systems, freeze configurations, fork testing processes, apply updates, and perform release management prototypes, this book shares how Microsoft Azure handles these common development tasks.

First of all, developers have to think of Microsoft Azure as a platform that supports MORE than just Microsoft focused services. While it was true that early renditions of Azure (once called "Windows Azure") was very Microsoft specific, under the leadership of Microsoft's new CEO, Satya Nadella, Microsoft, and specifically Microsoft Azure, extends far beyond just "Microsoft" based things.

As we will cover in this book, we'll be addressing non-Microsoft application services like Linux, Puppet, Chef, Docker, table-based data stores, and the like. We will go through the common lifecycle of Dev and Test in the real world, not solely how Microsoft envisions it, but how enterprises around the world manage their application lifecycle management across various platforms utilizing various tools.

The content of this book will share real world scenarios and best practices leveraged by development teams on a day to day basis that utilize Microsoft Azure to do in Microsoft's cloud what organizations have done for years in on-premise datacenters and test environments, but now leveraging the versatility and agility of the cloud.

Hopefully you will find this text helpful in framing Microsoft Azure in a manner that will ultimately allow you to decrease operational costs, and gain better control, release management, structure, and operational management of your Dev, Test, and DevOps services!

Part I:
Introducing (or Reintroducing) Azure for Dev and Test Environments

1 AZURE AS A DEV AND TEST PLATFORM

In this chapter, we will cover the framework of Microsoft Azure and how it can be leveraged as the target location to host Dev and Test systems, along with the Online tools available from Microsoft to assist in the application lifecycle management common in development environments.

Thinking of Azure Beyond PaaS and IaaS

The first step is to think of Microsoft Azure as a Dev and Test environment. Most individuals doing Dev and Test are aware that Microsoft Azure provides Platform as a Service (PaaS) as well as Infrastructure as a Service (IaaS) services, these are the roots of the Azure platform.

Microsoft still provides PaaS where organizations can simply upload their .NET Framework code to Azure and run their applications up in Azure. In fact Microsoft has expanded their PaaS offering and provides other PaaS services including allowing organizations to upload Microsoft SQL data, structured and unstructured database table data, Microsoft SharePoint data, and the like.

Or from a very raw IaaS perspective, Microsoft Azure allows organizations to build Windows Servers, Linux Servers, even upload their own virtual machines and run the entire VM up in Azure. As an IaaS hosting platform, an organization can remotely logon and completely control the configuration and operations of their VMs including enabling firewalls settings, configuring multiple virtual network adapters, setting up virtual storage ("C drives," "D drives," and the like), even mount ISO discs and install software onto the virtual machines.

And what many organizations are just realizing is that beyond Microsoft's Office 365 hosted Exchange email, Skype conferencing, and OneDrive storage, Microsoft provides an extensive library of Software as a Service (SaaS) applications within Azure. Some of the more common SaaS apps in Azure include Azure Machine Learning, where organizations can do predictive analysis modeling, Azure Active Directory, where organizations can leverage a cloud-based directory, even global enterprise application monitoring and performance analysis hosted by Microsoft Azure.

Because Microsoft provides PaaS, IaaS, and SaaS functionality in Azure, this is what makes it so powerful for enterprises doing Dev, Test, and DevOps that are looking for a hosted cloud solution. Rather than simply providing virtual machines, or simply providing cloud-based Application Lifecycle Management tools, or just providing PaaS hosted development environments, Microsoft provides ALL of these services from a single cloud administration console.

In fact, most enterprises end up using several of the Azure services in their Dev, Test, and DevOps environments because it is significantly easier to develop, deploy, monitor, track, support, and manage an enterprise class development environment when the services are all integrated.

Utilizing Microsoft's Strategy for Cloud-First Development

At the start of 2014, Microsoft's new Chief Executive Officer, Satya Nadella, came onboard and made a statement that Microsoft was changing from a Windows, Office, predominantly on-premise organizations to one that is "Cloud first and Mobile First" in its focus. Not that Microsoft has given up on developing and expanding their core platforms, but a whole new focus of the new Microsoft that supports any and every mainstream endpoint device with applications provided as a hosted cloud service.

Within 6 months of Nadella taking the helm of Microsoft, the organization was shipping Microsoft Office apps for the iPad, Android, and Apple Mac platforms. Microsoft went from being predominantly focused at hosting Windows Server virtual machines in their cloud environment to one that has fully embraced the hosting of Linux virtual machines, Oracle databases, and replicating VMWare virtual machines to their cloud environments.

Microsoft shifted from an organization that developed applications on-premise and eventually made them work in the cloud to an organization that started to release all of their applications and services in the Cloud first at an extremely rapid pace. New releases are coming out at least every 3-4 months, and sometimes releasing every few weeks, and when applicable the cloud features and services are being integrated into service packs and updates to on-premise environments.

Microsoft has truly become an enterprise focused on Cloud first development and release, at an Enterprise Cloud pace, offering services to non-Microsoft platform, application, and development environments, with an Annual R&D budget that rivals the Gross Domestic Product (GDP) of many nations. Microsoft has not only jumped in to the multi-platform development environment, but is providing functionality and services that would normally take integrating the services of dozens of disparate organizations together, however in the case of Microsoft, all of the functions and services are available right from within the main centralized Microsoft Azure console.

Enabling Microsoft Solutions for Microsoft Development

While we've set the stage to note that Microsoft Azure provides development environments for non-Microsoft platforms like Linux, Docker, Hadoop, GIT, and the like, for enterprises doing development with Microsoft platforms like .NET and SQL, it only makes sense that these enterprises are leveraging the full capabilities of Azure for their cloud-based development needs. Who can provide better cloud hosted services for Microsoft development environments better than Microsoft themselves.

And granted, it took Microsoft a couple extra cycles to get their cloud-hosted services in gear to provide the Dev and Test platform environment to the level and capacity that organizations wanted, now with Microsoft fully in the game, their services around Microsoft development cloud-based platforms is setting a high bar for top of the class standards.

Many of the mainstream services that development organizations have been most familiar with in the past like Visual Studios, Release Management for Visual Studio, and MSDN are now fully supported up in Microsoft Azure in the cloud. MSDN customers are provided monthly credits to host applications, leverage Azure SaaS applications, upload and run VMs, develop code, process change management, and the like all up in Azure.

Tools like Term Foundation Server (TFS) have been updated and put in a cloud-hosted SaaS model, now called Visual Studio Online (VSO). Even things like Release Management for Visual Studio is now offered as a SaaS solution, hosted as a cloud service.

5

So if you've done things in the past with on-premise tools, you can choose to CONTINUE to use updated releases of those tools and manage development environments both on-premise as well as now in Azure in the cloud, or switch to a completely cloud-hosted version of applications.

Extending On-premise Processes to Azure in the Cloud

As with most tools and services from Microsoft, organizations can choose a hybrid approach of having some resources and services on-premise, while other resources and services are in the cloud. Unlike most cloud service provides that are completely cloud-only, Microsoft's hybrid offering has been extremely helpful for enterprises to continue to leverage their investment in on-premise tools and services.

Organizations that have on-premise capacity to deploy virtual machines, host applications, test applications, even on-premise test tools don't have to throw out the on-premise investment. Microsoft Azure can be an extension for added capacity, or as on-premise resources are depreciated, start becoming unreliable, or not keeping up with the performance demands of the organization, enterprises can shift some capacity to the cloud. It is this hybrid flexibility that helps organizations leverage the cloud, while maintaining appropriate levels of function and services on-premise to meet the needs of the enterprise.

Leveraging the Agility of the Cloud

The key to the cloud has always been about agility and cost savings, which in early days of the cloud it was hard to truly see how the cloud was going to save costs and provide flexibility and agility. Much of the early cloud frustrations were the justification of the cloud due to costs to onboard to the cloud, plus the concern of downtime, security, and performance made the cloud a difficult choice in its infancy.

However now that we are years later, cloud providers like Microsoft have gotten past their early bumps and bruises of running an enterprise scale cloud, and cost savings have finally kicked in. Enterprises can now safely and reliably leverage the cloud, and hybrid models now allow organizations to simply extend on-premise functionality into the cloud.

As an enterprise that might be running 100, 500, 5000 VMs on-premise but might need 10%, 20%, 50% more capacity, rather than going out and buying more hardware, setting up more datacenter space, buying more storage, and hosting the growth in capacity on-premise, the cloud and the hybrid model now allows enterprises to extend that excess capacity need into the cloud.

And as the enterprise scales back capacity needs, potentially as a development cycle or season is over and a ramp down is appropriate, an organization can shutdown and eliminate development resources in the cloud and completely eliminate cloud operating costs for unused capacity. This is something that could never be done on-premise. When an organization bought $1-million worth of hardware and put it in their datacenter, they had and owned $1-million of hardware whether they used it or now. With the agility of the cloud, an organization can spin up 1,000 virtual machines one day when they need them, and the next day completely eliminate those VMs and not pay an extra cent toward the operation and management cost of those unneeded virtual machines.

2 AZURE BEYOND MICROSOFT WORKLOADS AND FUNCTIONALITY

While developers can understand Microsoft Azure having been designed to be a robust development environment for Microsoft platforms, what takes folks by surprise is how robust Azure is in supporting non-Microsoft platform environments. Microsoft has spent more in one-year on R&D in the development and support of non-Microsoft development platform services than it has over the past 3-years combined on their development of their Microsoft focused services. And it's not that Microsoft hasn't spent any money on Microsoft focused services, it's just that they had a lot of catching up to do when it came to supporting cloud-based non-Microsoft platforms.

Utilizing Azure for Linux-based Server Hosting

When we say that Microsoft supports Linux-based servers running in Azure, Microsoft has had support for Linux for some time now, however those who have tried to run Linux distributions in anything Microsoft in the past has always been challenged with core functionality that should work but just hasn't worked. Again, it's that shift of Microsoft from being an enterprise that simply says it does something, to an enterprise that actually has robust support for a platform and environment.

Microsoft Azure Supporting Linux Deployments

And while Microsoft's support of Linux is significantly better than what it was just a few months ago, the evolution of Linux support, and Microsoft's offerings around Linux backup, customization, management, monitoring, automated provisioning, and the like is expanding at exponential rates. In fact there are things that can be done with Linux distributions in Azure that Microsoft has yet to release for Windows Server images. So the Linux team at Microsoft has a huge push to ensure that Linux on Azure is a widely supported full and robust offering.

Leveraging Azure Tables for Limitless Data Repositories

Beyond just the fundamentals of virtual machines in a non-Windows platform environment, Microsoft provides data storage in Azure. But not simply just Microsoft SQL server for data storage, but directly addressable tables stored as data objects. These Azure Tables allow organizations the ability to create and store a limitless amount of information in Azure, and directly address the content without having to depend solely on the structure of SQL.

Many organizations use these Azure Tables to quickly store data coming in from data acquisition devices, information streaming from "Internet of Things" endpoints, managing analytic data, and the like. Tables can be quickly setup, fields added and changed, and data consumed directly from applications.

Utilizing Azure Event Hubs for Frontend Scalability

Azure Event Hubs is a Platform as a Service "frontend" environment in Azure that allows developers to utilize Microsoft's Event Hubs stream processing in the Azure cloud. Developers can focus on creating endpoint apps and backend data systems, and leave the data-stream ingestion process to Azure to manage.

The Azure Event Hub service is commonly used by organizations that have a large number of endpoints or input sources that is looking to simplify the input streaming of information. Developers can leverage the capability of the Azure Event Hubs in a manner that helps the organization more quickly scale to the demands of their information access requirements without having to setup virtual frontend servers, deal with server load balancing, and have to manage redundancy and scalability.

Leveraging Azure Data Factory for Data Aggregation

Azure Data Factory is another cloud-based service that helps organizations more quickly and easily aggregate, analyze, and manage their data. Azure Data Factory starts with its ability to connect to data stored in Azure, Azure SQL, even on-premise SQL servers. Once connected to the data sources, Azure Data Factory provides organizations the ability to create, orchestrate, and manage their data processing pipeline, and then transform the data into a more commonly accessed common data responsibility for management by business intelligence and analytics tools.

Again, Azure provides organizations the ability to more rapidly access information and analyze the information leveraging cloud resources than simply taking structure databases that are running on-premise and moving the exact same systems to the cloud. For organizations truly looking to change the way they manage, access, manipulate, assess, and analyze data, Azure has innovative tools in terms of Azure Tables, Azure Event Hubs, and Azure Data Factory that helps organizations rethink and redeploy business focused services to meet the capacity and scale of the cloud.

Accessing Structure Data through Azure Stream Analytics

Azure Stream Analytics is an event processing engine that extracts data from "Internet of Things" endpoints like devices, sensors, acquisition devices, databases, or data resources in real time and provide analytics of the data. Azure Stream Analytics supports the ingestion of millions of events.

Instead of spending time setting up hardware and building data warehouses, Azure Stream Analytics allows developers the ability to simply create a SQL-based query syntax, run it against the acquired data, and run analytic sequences against the data. Microsoft Azure handles the scale, performance, redundancy, and resiliency of the data and scale of the data

Utilizing Azure Batch for Parallel Processing Solutions

For organizations that have data transaction needs that are best run in batches, Azure Batch provides large scale parallel processing of information without the organization's need to build server farms, clusters, connectivity, cooling, power redundancy, network redundancy, and the like.

Developers can stage data to Azure, build job-execution pipelines, and deliver self-service applications as a service. Azure Batch is yet another cloud-based service that Microsoft provides to developers in a creative manner of allowing for cloud scale, redundancy, resiliency, and management without the need to develop, implement, and manage the datacenter infrastructure typically required of large scale application environments.

3 KEY BENEFITS OF AZURE COMPARED TO AMAZON WEB SERVICES

As organizations look to scale their development systems to the cloud, many have already begun their usage of Amazon Web Services as their target cloud provider. Amazon no doubt did a better job than Microsoft in providing an open, heterogeneous cloud platform environment that organizations with a mix of Windows and non-Windows platforms were able to easily leverage.

However with Microsoft greatly expanding its services to support the broad platform base that enterprise developers use, Microsoft has been able to win back the mindshare of developers with a better holistic approach to the cloud than what Amazon provides.

Providing More than Just a Hosted Platform but an Entire Development Platform

Amazon is for the most part just a cloud hosting environment. Organizations can setup virtual machines up in Azure as well as build out applications leveraging Amazon's hosted Websites and cloud platform offering.

However key to Microsoft's offering is that Microsoft does more than just provide the basic platform. Microsoft has been in the development tools business from its very beginning several decades ago. For organizations using Visual Studios or any other Microsoft development and management tool, Microsoft Azure has exceptional support for these tools to manage resources in their Azure cloud environment.

For organizations building applications for Windows-based systems, Microsoft makes the core Windows operating system, and thus their ability to develop and manage applications in Azure is something that is native integration to Azure.

Additionally, Microsoft provides monitoring and management tools in their System Center suite of offerings that snap right into Azure and provides organizations a full end to end solution for application development, management, hosting, security, and support.

This extension of Microsoft's operating system, hypervisor, development tools, and management tools to Azure provides Microsoft a significant advantage over someone like Amazon that focuses primarily on cloud hosting. End of the day, it's about the tools and management of the development environment that is critical to day to day development tasks, and that the hosted platform is just a target location where information is stored.

With Microsoft providing a comparable hosted cloud target environment, it's all of the other things that Microsoft provides that has made enterprises look to Microsoft as the full provider of cloud-based applications and services.

Maximizing the Use of Common Microsoft-based On-premise Tools and Resources

Development teams that have worked with traditional Microsoft-based development tools like Visual Studios, or management tools like Team Foundation Server, will find that these tools have been updated over the past year or two and are now fully supportive of Microsoft Azure and cloud services.

Visual Studio 2013 provide connectivity to Microsoft Azure, and with the release of Visual Studio 2015, Microsoft will have a full new release built specifically to support the development and management of applications within Azure.

While Visual Studio has full integrated support for Azure, these tools also have full support for developing applications on-premise. Organizations don't need to learn new tools, they don't need to develop new processes, developers can simply take what they've been doing for year's on-premise and add the cloud as a target destination for code deployment. This helps organizations quickly onboard cloud services and scale to the cloud without having to redo how they do everything.

And for organizations that have been using Team Foundation Server on-premise to manage their application lifecycle processes, TFS is now Visual Studio Online, and is a cloud-hosted software as a service offering by Microsoft. Visual Studio Online helps organizations develop applications, work as teams, manage their code, manage bugs, communicate and collaborate as a team in a unified manner.

Combined with Release Management for Visual Studio as a hosted online service, Microsoft has solidified the end to end development lifecycle for organizations with robust tools.

For organizations that have been using these tools for some time now in on-premise development processes, simply shifting to cloud-based versions of the tools, and/or leveraging Microsoft Azure as the target development repository helps organizations leverage the agility of the cloud, while utilizing familiar tools and applications.

Extending the Use of Non-Microsoft-based On-premise Tools and Resources

However for organizations that aren't using Microsoft tools for development and management, with recent changes by Microsoft to fully embrace and support non-Microsoft based solutions, Microsoft Azure can now support a wide range of offerings.

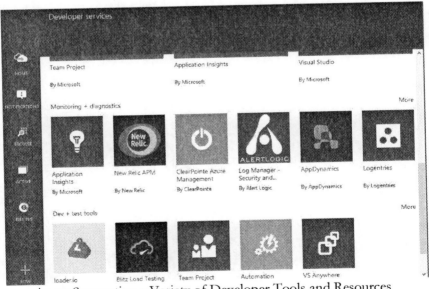

Azure Supporting a Variety of Developer Tools and Resources

Some of the non-Microsoft based platform and service support solutions being supported today includes virtual machines running Linux, support for Puppet and Chef to manage Azure-based systems and applications, the ability for developers to use things like Docker and Docker Hub for development, the integration and use of GIT, and the like. This book will cover these non-Microsoft tools and technologies in upcoming chapters to drill down in more detail how enterprises are leveraging the tools in a Microsoft Azure environment with full functionality and services.

Leveraging the Microsoft Azure Marketplace for App Store Extensibility

Extending beyond traditional Microsoft tools and Azure-based hosted offerings, Microsoft also has a very robust marketplace for developers to download and integrate apps into their development processes.

Some of the 3rd party apps that are available up in the Microsoft Azure App Store include apps that enable code signing, graphic library apps, multimedia tool integration apps, coding helper apps, and the like. Developers can pick and choose apps to work with as a mechanism to hopefully simplify their development tasks.

As a comparative to Amazon or other cloud providers, being that Microsoft has an extensive resource base of developers, the Microsoft's app store for Azure is growing extensively as Microsoft's partner community continues to develop components that can be shared with others.

Part II:
Enabling Microsoft's Application Lifecycle Management Processes into Azure in the Cloud

4 SERVING THE APPLICATION OWNER

As those working with application lifecycle management and application development know, there are generally two major leads in the effort, the Application Owner and the Datacenter Administrator. This chapter will address the needs of the first lead, the Application Owner.

Providing Flexible Systems for Development

The Application Owner is the lead on the application development initiative who as the job title identifies is the person focused on the application, works with the users of the application, and typically oversees or even is the developer of the application. The Application Owner is generally involved in the self-provisioning, innovation, and experimentation process of the application.

In the self-provisioning process, the Application Owner works the closest with the Datacenter Administrator as is most interested in the process of having the application development environment available to build, test, and manage code. The Application Owner typically identifies what development language, tools, and application lifecycle management process is expected, and the Datacenter Administrator builds and supports the environment. There's usually a fair amount of interaction between the Application Owner and the Datacenter Administrator to fine tune the environment and the services that the Datacenter Administrator will provide to the Application Owner.

The Application Owner then spends their time innovating and experimenting with the development of their application. While it may seem like a routine process of code development and traditional lifecycle management of the evolution of the code, it's the most creative Application Owners that try our new or better processes to come up with not only an expected end result of the code, but also something that is truly better, improved, and worthy of users to buy, implement, migrate, and/or be happy with the new software once is it rolled out.

This innovation takes experimentation in trying different things, validating that they work, confirming that what was planned and expected achieved the anticipated results. The interaction with the development environment is the highest in this process as the application code is rolled out in a Dev process, tests are performed, good code is retained, buggy states are frozen to be debugged and fixed, code states are branched, and changes go through iterative processes.

Minimizing the Learning Curve

In the development process, time is always of essence, and in this world of the cloud, it seems like we took the fast pace development cycle of "Internet time" and further accelerated it to "cloud time." For enterprises to develop and release code quickly, it is usually preferred to use the tools and processes that developers are most familiar with. The development language is usually not a decision of any of the developers or the Application Owner, it is set in the original state of the application itself, whether that's .NET, Python, C#, Perl, or the like. But many times there are options in the development process, change control tools, and management tools when it comes to things like Visual Studio, Team Foundation Server, GIT, Puppet, Chef, or the like.

There are times when enterprises choose to utilize a different process management or application lifecycle management tool with many organizations making that shift these days to cloud-based Software as a Service applications. The shift, while requiring developers to work with a different tool, helps the organization be more nimble in the fast paced code development, review, approval, and stakeholder acceptance process. The changes experienced by the developers is typically minimal as the SaaS-based tools are based on well-known and experienced processes, so it's just a matter of working with something that is the same, but slightly different.

Accelerating Deployment Cycles

As part of the accelerated development process, enterprises have always leveraged standard templates, images, and rapid provisioning processes.

This is where the cloud had evolved the most and has provided developers the ability to leverage the scale and agility of the cloud.

With on-premise development environments, users working in different locations from primary development databases frequently did not benefit from standard templates and images. Or due to development system capacity, development images had to be eliminated more rapidly than desired so that branches in code had to be revised, merged, and solidified much sooner than desired.

With the virtually unlimited capacity of the cloud, the application lifecycle management process could extend from an application taking up hundreds of images to one that is utilizing the various stages of thousands or tens of thousands of states and images. This has provided more flexibility in a fast paced development environment.

And with the cloud, rapid provisioning has helped developers build new images and new system states without the constraints of existing on-premise hardware or old hardware that has gotten sluggish over the years. The cloud capacity and the cloud performance is a great benefit in the development cycle for developers.

Facilitating Powerful Tools for Testing

Beyond just writing code, a significant step in the application lifecycle process involves load testing, freezing, snapshotting, and merging code. Again, thanks to the agility and virtually limitless capacity of the cloud environment, plus tools and resources built in to Microsoft Azure, there are plenty of options for developers to expand their testing of their applications.

Integral to Visual Studios Online as well as in many other application development platforms that work with Microsoft Azure is functionality that allows code bases to be forked and merged as required of the application development and testing process.

From a development operations perspective, Microsoft Azure provides robust capabilities to snapshot virtual machines, and integrates with lifecycle management tools to freeze code bases and work on various branches of the code as deemed appropriate for the development of the application.

Leveraging Agility in the Cloud

And as has been mentioned several times already in this chapter is the agility of the cloud, to be able to expand capacity to a virtually limitless scale, and then scale back and only pay for capacity in use. Gone are the days of buying excess capacity of hardware, only to have it obsolete in a couple years or deemed to not be enough capacity to meet the needs of the development lifecycle.

Microsoft Azure provides developers as much capacity that is needed on a "pay by the minute" granularity so that capacity is used and eliminated on demand.

5 ASSISTING THE DATACENTER ADMINISTRATOR

The other lead in the application lifecycle process is the Datacenter Administrator, who works hand in hand with the Application Owner in developing, facilitating, and managing the infrastructure used in the development of applications. It is the Datacenter Administrators role to provide enough capacity, automate tasks and sequences, and maintain the operations of the compute, storage, networking, security, and availability of the development environment.

As development workloads are moved to the cloud, the Datacenter Administrator's role changes. In an on-premise development environment, the Datacenter Administrator built hardware, patched operating systems, provided redundancy and clustering, and backed up systems. However in the cloud world, there are no longer servers and systems to manage, however providing resiliency and security is still a core task of the Datacenter Administrator.

While the Datacenter Administrator no longer has to work with hardware, it doesn't mean the Datacenter Administrator is twiddling their thumbs with nothing to do. In fact, the evolution to the cloud for application development has enhanced the role of the Datacenter Administrator. Instead of building and configuring hardware, and managing blinking lights, the Datacenter Administrator has a more critical role in optimizing the experience and services that can be provided to the Application Owner.

The Datacenter Administrator can now develop templates and images, automate tasks, create self-service portals, and truly transform the hosted cloud from being just a platform for applications, to being an optimized environment for development.

Providing Standard Template Images

The process of building standard template images that developers can work from is nothing new in the Datacenter Administration process. However what has drastically improved is the method of creating templates. For organizations that have been using automation tools on-premise in the past, like using something like Microsoft System Center Virtual Machine Manager, the organization can leverage existing images and templates, and by simply using the latest releases of the VMM tool, can automate the creation of images up in Azure in the cloud.

Alternately, Microsoft Azure has standard templates in its Template Gallery that users can choose from and have those templates deployed in a few minutes. Standard templates include base Windows Server and Linux operating system templates to fully operational SQL Server and SharePoint Server templates, ready to be customized as a user chooses.

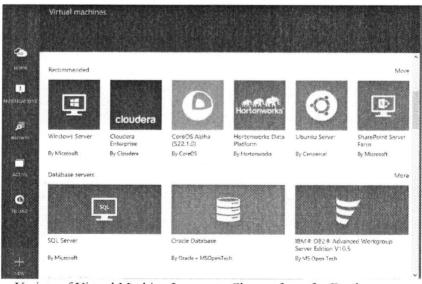

Variety of Virtual Machine Images to Choose from for Deployment

Templates can also be created straight from PowerShell command line sequences, including not only building the base image, but injecting in application services, Windows features, and customizing the configuration of the image. PowerShell is a powerful command line tool that allows an organization to pipe in custom settings from a text file, and repeatedly deploy identical configurations without variation or user error.

Simplifying Service Level Agreements

As noted, the Datacenter Administrator no longer has to build servers, build out secondary datacenters, cluster servers, replicate systems between datacenters, distribute workloads, or all of the tasks that used to take up the time of several full time personnel. Instead, the Datacenter Administrator can leverage the capabilities of Microsoft's Azure cloud, and set default policies and configure template standards that meet the expectations of the developers.

By default, Azure workloads are redundant within a datacenter so that if a host server that an application or image is running on fails, there's at least one additional system in the datacenter that'll provide redundant and resilient uptime. Organizations may want to extend the redundancy of applications and services by enabling geo-redundancy of their images. Geo-redundancy extends the local replication to include at least a second datacenter so that in the event that a datacenter fails, the system image and/or application is replicated and available in a secondary center.

Beyond just image redundancy, organizations have the ability of creating multiple network segments and isolated replicated storage of information, again, all in the process of maintaining resiliency of content. The great thing about the Microsoft Azure cloud is that this redundancy is simply a checkbox or a deployment script line command to enable the resiliency. Instead of the on-premise responsibility of actually building datacenters and the underlying redundancy and replication of applications, content, storage, and fabric needed, the Datacenter Administrator can focus on other important business and data responsibilities.

Managing Licensing

As enterprises deploy images in Microsoft Azure, Microsoft has a couple different costing models for running system images. For organizations running Windows images, SQL Server images, or SharePoint images, the cost of the licensing for each of the servers is included in the runtime cost of the cloud-based system. So if the cost to run an image is 4.5-cents a minute, that operating cost includes the Windows Server license running on the image. For organizations running a non-Microsoft operating system, a lower cost is associated to the running of the image that does not include the Windows Server license.

This embedded licensing cost to the runtime of the image helps organizations with server licensing, so instead of counting the number of running systems, adding up active and inactive images, auditing systems, and the like, simply turning on and running a system in Azure includes the appropriate software license cost for the system.

Control Deployment and Operations Costs

In addition to Microsoft Azure including the licensing cost in the runtime operations of system images, Microsoft Azure, as noted, provides high availability as part of the runtime cost. For additional operational services like backup and disaster recovery, organizations can also leverage Azure services to address these deployment and operational controls.

For backup, Microsoft has Azure Backup that provides organizations the ability to not only take snapshots of images, but to backup the images to digital storage, just as if the organization were backing up systems to digital or tape medium on-premise. Through the use of something like Windows Backup, to more sophisticated backup solutions like Microsoft's System Center Data Protection Manager or even third party backup tools, organizations can make backups of their systems on an ongoing basis.

For Disaster Recovery, Microsoft Azure has services such as Azure Site Recovery (ASR) that replicates images between on-premise datacenters and Azure. ASR can be leveraged as a migration technology to replicate running systems on-premise to the Azure cloud, and then "failover" the running system off of the on-premise environment to then run in the Azure environment. This is an easy way for an organization to replicate templates, backup running application systems, and move critical business systems from on-premise to Azure.

Additionally, enterprises can choose to replicate content from Azure back down to an on-premise image so that if an organization wants to move off the cloud environment, they can just as easily replicate back to the on-premise data, then failover from the Cloud back to on-premise. ASR provides a number of scenarios for simply replicating content between on-premise and Azure, or Azure and on-premise, and failover and failback instances as needed.

These tasks are key components that help organizations leverage the capabilities of Datacenter Administration tasks, but through services provided by Microsoft in Azure. Instead of having to buy, build, implement, and manage physical servers, physical networking equipment, physical storage systems as has been done for years on-premise, organizations can shift their datacenter management responsibilities.

Providing Governance

Lastly, in a world where security, regulatory compliance, and standard processes are critical, leveraging Microsoft Azure also offloads Datacenter Administrators from the task of repeatedly going through audits, reviews, and remediation of on-premise centers, and instead simply request the audit reports and 3rd party audit reviews that Microsoft readily makes available to its customers.

Microsoft's Azure datacenters go through stringent audits, and ongoing certifications, with documented reviews and comments on everything from compliance with HIPAA, SOC 1, SOC 2, PCI, EU DPD, and the like. More information is provided in the section of this book on security, as Microsoft leverages its Azure cloud to be a reliable, dependable, and secure environment.

Microsoft knows that its success and organizations adoption of Azure is based on Microsoft's ability to secure, protect, and manage their datacenters. Failure to meet the trust and expectations of enterprises can spell the failure of Microsoft to retain customers and attract new customers to their services, thus Microsoft heavily invests in the ongoing protection of their environment.

6 UTILIZING FOUNDATIONAL APPLICATION LIFECYCLE MANAGEMENT TO MANAGE PROJECTS

Besides writing and producing code, the system involved in the development process involving a solid application lifecycle management (ALM) solutions is key to the managed development and release of code. This chapter covers some of the tools available in the ALM process, and standard practices leveraged by development teams.

Starting with an Application Lifecycle Management Tool

For development teams, there are several options available in managing the lifecycle of application development in Microsoft Azure. A common platform leveraged by many enterprises has been Microsoft's Team Foundation Server (TFS), which has been an on-premise tool that manages code, annotates releases, and provides a platform for collaboration and communications between developers.

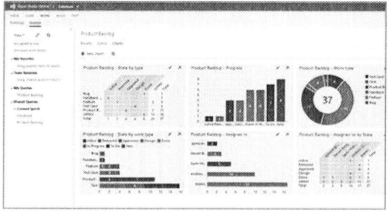

Microsoft Team Foundation Server – Reporting View

As enterprises began to leverage Microsoft Azure as the target to host code development and management of releases, Microsoft released a hosted application lifecycle management tool, Visual Studio Online. Visual Studio Online provides similar functionality as TFS, however as a Software as a Service offering.

More specific details on feature comparison between TFS and Visual Studio Online is provided on Microsoft's site at:

http://www.visualstudio.com/en-us/products/compare-visual-studio-products-vs.aspx

Building the Dev/Test Hosted Environment

While this book focuses on Dev, Test, and DevOps as it relates to Microsoft's Azure in the cloud, many enterprises are still doing development on-premise, and it would be presumptuous to believe that an organization would immediately switch all development overnight into the cloud.

One of the benefits of Microsoft Azure is that it provides a hybrid model where some development can be done on-premise, and other development done in Azure in the cloud. When using tools like recent releases of Visual Studio, Visual Studio Online, or Team Foundation Server, the tools provide management of development both on-premise as well as in Azure.

When building environments on-premise, enterprises are familiar with the process that involves setting up datacenters, installing racks, mounting host servers, building virtual machine templates, deploying images, and making available an application development environment for developers to build and test their code. As noted previously in this book, leveraging

Microsoft Azure in the cloud eliminates the core infrastructure aspects of building out datacenters and physical development environments, allowing development teams and datacenter administrators to start right in on application lifecycle management processes.

The focus for cloud-based environments is less on the systems, and more time spent on code development, which is what it should be for development teams. Instead of building systems, effort is focused on code development optimization, team communications, and release management.

Writing and Sharing Code

Core to application lifecycle management is the writing and sharing of code. There are several options available to developers, leveraging things like the Team Foundation Version Control system that is part of Team Foundation Server and Visual Studio Online, or using a distributed system like GIT.

TF Version Control is centralized, so processes, workflow, collaboration, management, and operational controls are integrated into Team Foundation Server of Visual Studio Online. Being that it is integrated into the application lifecycle management tool, separate processes are not required.

Many development teams are already using GIT and may be writing and sharing code within workgroups or individualized teams. Code and release management of code is based on the approval processes and systems identified by the teams, with some form of external communications (frequently email or these days social media collaboration platforms) that allow distributed teams to work in a pseudo-collaborative manner.

Establishing a Code Development Process

During the code development process, there's a need to branch, merge, freeze, and visualize the code in its various states and form. The application lifecycle management process needs to take in account the processes in which code can evolve in this manner.

As code is developed, there will be times when a certain version of the code needs to be frozen, either to look for a problem within the code, or to freeze the code when it has been quality assurance tested and validated as being solid. In the case of freezing for bug analysis, code is held in a state and is then thoroughly reviewed and tested to isolate a problem. This can take several parallel instances of the code to isolate the problem, and where the agility of the cloud comes in handy. Developers can spin up multiple instances of the code, sometimes hundreds of instances to have enough testers work through the code to find the problem.

Freezing the code base for good code is always preferred, and from this state, a new branch (a good branch) of the code takes shape. There may be a point where the code needs to be rolled back to a branch in the base to roll back to an earlier state, thus maintaining older releases of the code allows for the flexibility to look at various states of the code during the development process.

As multiple teams work together, code may need to be merged and combined, with various branches joined together. The merging of code requires further historical instances of the code as debugging needs to take place across all sections of the code to ensure that the merging of the code did not inject any problems between code sets.

And throughout the code development process as code is branched and merged, having a good virtual view of the state of the code that would allow the development team leads to identify all of the various states of the code is important. If the code base needs to be rolled back, that there would be a visual cue to help the management team determine where code was branched, merged, frozen, rolled back, and revised.

It is a lengthy and tedious process as code is developed, and even more so important for large teams and complex code where multiple teams are collaborating together in the development, test, and merging of the code. Good application lifecycle management processes are important to ensure the overall success of the development of the application.

Managing Code Development

While branching, merging, and managing code is important, the overall application lifecycle management process requires a clear definition, priority, and assignment of the tasks of the development of the code. These management tasks are important for those managing the code development. Having an application lifecycle management tool that assists in this process supports the production management team.

The management team wants to be able to track backlogs and focus the development teams to work in sprints. The sprints break down the development cycle into shorter and more manageable sequences. As multiple teams are in various states of their code, the backlog can be viewed to determine the state of the development, so that as code is being developed, there's a clear demarcation what state the various teams are at.

During the development cycle, it is helpful to link work items to code changes. The visualization of the changes to the state of the work allows a validation that core expectations are met.

7 WORKING AS A TEAM IN APPLICATION DEVELOPMENT

Small application development projects with just a single developer is easy to track the effort of an individual with a little bit of time and sequence tracking. However when an application development effort involves multiple teams working on different branches of the code base, or even different developers working on different parts of the same branch of the code base, it becomes extremely important that the team efforts are well communicated among the developers.

Planning Projects and Tracking Work Efforts

Successful team development involves effective collaboration and tracking of processes. Organizations have used various on-premise tools over the years, however when teams are distributed across multiple geographic locations, or in many cases developers are working from home or in remote locations, having the right tool is important.

Over the past 2-3 years, what has been found to be effective in social networking technologies has been the inherent cloud-based social media communications tools, and those same concepts have been evolved to help development teams communicate and collaborate across wide distances to work together in the development of code. Software as a Service application lifecycle management tools help development teams collaborate, track, and visualize the state of work efforts. Code is tagged for categorization, and filters are used to identify the state of tags.

Managing Tasks and Coordinating Efforts of the Team

In working with team efforts, the ability to assign tasks, assign bug remediation, track status, and coordinate efforts is important. Through the application lifecycle management process, being able to identify the developers and assign priority responsibility of certain tasks to an individual allows for the distribution of workloads. Holistically viewing the status of all tasks and assignments enables the management to know the load of work as well as the state of the completion of the tasks.

As bugs are identified, they too can be tasked to individuals to manage and/or to remediate the code. Task level sequences can be invoked to review the code and work through the bug, with code changes tracked and further quality assurance testing performed to validate that the problem has been addressed. Status across each task can be addressed, rolled up to a single view, and ensured that all efforts of all development team members are successfully coordinated.

Using Portfolio Management to Bring Together Group Efforts

Many development teams use a portfolio management approach to coordinate the efforts of a team. Some development teams use a Scrum approach to work through development cycles, from collaborating on tasks that need to be completed, to distributing work efforts in squashing bugs and advancing the code line sequences.

The tracking and management of code leverages things like a Kanban board to better visualize the state of group efforts, post notes and ideas, share the state of development through a dashboard approach, and more effectively communicate development operations.

Every developer has worked through different methods and processes, and it is up to the development management team to set a process, communicate to the team how the process will flow, and coordinate the efforts of the developers through the process.

With cloud-based apps and solutions, development teams can leverage management systems in the cloud that provide integration with various Kanban board, Scrum processes, and collaborative and open communications systems that link teams in various development locations together in a virtual development center. The options are greater these days to leverage the cloud not only as a target to store code, but to also manage the process of code development efforts.

Using Kanban Board to Manage Development Efforts

As noted in the previous section, a Kanban board is frequently used to manage development efforts. The Kanban board can track progress, focus a team on the tasks at hand, and track the progress of various sprints in the development cycle. From a centralized view, to a distributed task view, progress tracking can provide stakeholders the information they need to understand the status of the development efforts. The Kanban board can also roll up tasks and visually provide a status of efforts for each developer to a development manager of the progress of the team.

Stakeholders can be invited to review the status of a project, whether that's reviewing backlogs or simply seeing a single page dashboard. The Kanban board can help to visualize a taskbar or counter that notes the number of open bugs, the progress of each team member, and the overall state of the project.

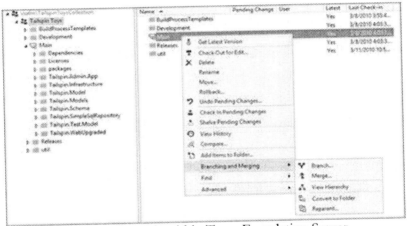

Version Controls within Team Foundation Server

The Kanban board can also be a centralized comment and suggestion medium, where various members and stakeholders can post comments and suggestions for view by others on the team. Comments can be assigned to specific individuals or teams to view and address, or they can be open to be viewed by several members of the team.

Utilizing Dashboards for Communications

As much as a development team can leverage an application lifecycle management tool for granular communication between team members and the development lead, having a centralized dashboard that rolls up communications is always helpful. A single dashboard that provides an overview can assist stakeholders to view information at a glance. The dashboard may be color coded with green, yellow, and red status indicators.

The visual snapshot can also roll up several projects into a single view so that a stakeholder responsible for multiple project efforts can see work across multiple efforts. These dashboards have replaced weekly email reports (that no one looks at) and instead provides a common view of the state of efforts of one or more teams.

8 LEVERAGING THE CLOUD UTILIZING VISUAL STUDIO ONLINE MANAGEMENT

So far in this book we've talked about application lifecycle management and the various tasks and processes followed during the development cycle. As many organizations are familiar with common on-premise tools for management, whether that's Team Foundation Server, GIT, or the like, as has been noted, as organizations shift their development platform to cloud targets like Microsoft Azure, there's also a movement to shift the tools used by development teams to cloud-based tools. Microsoft has shifted their tool base solution from Team Foundation Server to Visual Studio Online.

Hosting Code in the Cloud

The movement of management tools to cloud-based solutions eliminates the need for developers to have to setup on-premise servers and figure out how to get distributed teams access to an in-house server. Cloud-based tools inherently provide access from "anywhere", and provide a virtually limitless scale to meet the demands of development teams of all sizes.

In fact for small development teams, Microsoft has made Visual Studio Online available to teams of 5 or fewer members at no charge. This provides teams the ability to experience the online cloud application lifecycle management solution to determine whether it meets the needs of a small project, which could then be extended to larger scale efforts.

Centralizing the Management of Projects

Web-based solutions inherently provide support for distributed and virtual teams. As organizations have specialists in multiple locations, the ability to access the skills of those specialists in an overall effort adds to the value of the effort in progress. In the past, development teams have used distributed management tools since centralized tools were difficult to share across multiple regions. While this distributed management approach worked in the past, the challenge was distributed teams had a hard time truly understanding the state of a project.

So the centralization of the application lifecycle management tool brings together communications, collaboration, work effort, code branching, code base, comments, and suggestions. Stakeholders, managers, and development team members can, at a glance, know the state of a project or series of projects.

Enabling the Simplicity of Software as a Service

Having the application lifecycle management tool centralized not only has the benefits of bringing together distributed teams into a centralized communications model, but the Software as a Service model eliminates development teams from the burden of managing and administering "servers" that host the software. Application development teams should be focused on developing and managing code, not setting up application management software and code hosting servers.

Visual Studio Online – Managing Backlogs

The Software as a Service model eliminates the need of the development team from wasting cycles on the tools, and allows for more time to be allocated in the development of the code specific to the application project. Also, the SaaS model provides development teams with an ever evolving and developing tool. Instead of being stuck with a tool and "all that it

38

does", as the developer of the SaaS-based ALM tool looks to improve the tool with new features and functions, the development team benefits from the ongoing enhancements.

Those working in the SaaS application model are very aware of all of the benefits of SaaS applications, and the shift to a hosted model for not only code and image storage, but also for application lifecycle management tools is the direction of the industry.

Supporting Development Environments as Desired by Organizations

Although Visual Studio Online provides the integration of Team Foundation version control, development teams that might be using GIT can continue to use GIT as the integration of version controlling has integrated support for external methods and solutions. Even within the development environment, the development team can use template galleries that are provided as part of Microsoft's Azure cloud services, or a development team can bring in their own images, applications, and code and manage the version controls and codebase independently. The Azure cloud along with Microsoft's Visual Studio Online has been developed with the understanding that development teams have been using other tools and systems in the past, and that the best way to draw adoption to the Microsoft service offering is to be open for the integration of external solutions.

Monitoring Status Using Kanban or Agile Task Boards

As was highlighted in the last chapter, Kanban or Agile task boards are commonly used in development environments to allow centralized view of the status of a project or series of projects. Visual Studio Online has built in the Kanban board and the integration of the Agile task board so that development teams can create single view dashboards for their project or projects.

The task boards can be used to track the progress of sprints, allows developers and stakeholders to comment on projects, and provide view (and edit/comment) privileges based on varying levels of security levels.

Building Application in the Cloud

With Visual Studio Online, development teams can build, distribute, view, and manage processes throughout the lifecycle of the development efforts. Automation can be invoked to initiate the compilation and testing process of applications in the cloud. As part of various task sequences, a next step task can be initiated that helps advance efforts.

As an example, upon the approval of a codebase, an automation sequence can be initiated to distribute the new codebase to new images, potentially kicked off at night so that by the morning, all development systems have the new codebase. Older code bases can still exist, again, a benefit of the agility of the cloud of keeping older instances with virtually limitless capacity, however rather than losing a day or even a few hours while new images are released, automated processes can kick off and prepare the development environment with minimal user interaction.

Responding Faster to Development Cycles Through Automation

Automation has become the key differentiator in the effectiveness of a development lifecycle. As noted in the previous section, the automated distribution of images can prepare the development platform so that coders can immediately begin working on the most current and approved codebase.

Automation is also used in the testing and reporting processes where test tools can be launched to scan code and build code reports automatically rather than waiting for someone to initiate the code scanning process. These automation scans can also centralize the posting of report analysis for shared access on the platform dashboard for team members and stakeholders to access and view.

And when necessary, code can be redeployed through automation such as in instances where a rollback of code is needed, and all systems need to be rolled back to a common state. As code is merged, the importance of working on the same codebase is best facilitated in a structured and managed manner. Automation helps development teams with the task of keeping structured and well managed code, without the need for individual user intervention.

9 UTILIZING THE POWER OF RELEASE MANAGEMENT FOR VISUAL STUDIO

Application Lifecycle Management also includes a very important task of release management. Microsoft has had its Team Foundation Server and Release Management for Visual Studio as on-premise tools for years. And as has been mentioned several times already in this book, Team Foundation Server is now available as Visual Studio Online as a cloud-based Software as a Service model. Release Management for Visual Studio (http://www.visualstudio.com/en-us/products/release-management-for-microsoft-visual-studio-vs.aspx) has also been ported to the Microsoft cloud as a SaaS application, so development teams can now take advantage of Release Management for Visual Studio in the cloud.

Automating Multi-Stage Deployments using Release Management for Visual Studio

Release Management for Visual Studio allows development teams to visually create the configuration path of a project, and track the state of a deployment. This is especially critical in multi-stage deployments where interim releases are frozen and distributed to testing teams to perform various states of quality assurance testing against the code.

Release Management for Visual Studio – Multistage Management

While Visual Studio Online provides a more granular bug reporting and management system, the roll-up of the state of all code development aligns with the overall release management cycle of the project.

Release Management for Visual Studio automatically (and manually) triggers releases upon completion and approval of builds. Various steps can be defined with clear release notification processes. Release triggering can tie into automation processes that lock and roll out the codebase to development systems, ensuring all developers are working on the most current platform.

Supporting Multi-Platform Deployments

With Release Management for Visual Studio, while some might think that the Microsoft tool would only support Windows-based deployments, quite the contrary. Release Management for Visual Studio can manage the processes for projects involving Windows Server, Linux, Windows client, Windows Phone, Web application projects, and more. Release management is release management, you're tracking people, processes, timelines, feedback, and workflows, so the application being developed (and released) has little to do with platform of the code.

Running Automated Validation Tests During the Application Testing Lifecycle

Digging into the core functionality of Release Management for Visual Studios, developers want the ability to manage approval workflows, define approvers, manage approval notifications, trace tests, document bug fixes and notes, audit release trails, and the like. It's about tracking, managing, and releasing of code, as such the tool covers the full management aspects common in the release management workflow process.

Developers can stage controls through a Web portal or through the Release Management client, they can pause a deployment for manual steps and intervention, they can redirect processes, override workflows, and change processes based on changes in the work schedule.

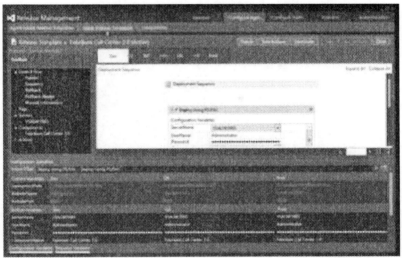

Release Management for Visual Studio Online – Staging Controls

Staging an Application Deployment Scenario Before Rolling it Into Production

Applications rarely go from initial development straight to production, there's almost always a staged process to bring the Development environment into a Test environment before rolling into Production. And in many enterprises, even the Test environment might stage yet once more into a pre-production environment before rolling into production, so there's a phased process.

With Microsoft Azure as a potential target destination for code development, developers may actually develop their application up in Azure (along with testing and validating code in Azure), with the production release in Azure or on-premise. Other enterprises may do all of their development on-premise in existing and traditional development environments, and then do Test or Production deployments up in Azure.

Azure is extremely flexible where it could be Dev, Test, or Production, and with hybrid cross support and integration between on-premise environments and Azure, developers have great flexibility in choosing the option of Cloud or on-premise that works best in their lifecycle.

Throughout the staging process, the lifecycle management process might have the environment roll-forward, but also roll-back updates and changes, and again it doesn't matter whether the content started in the cloud and published on-prem, or started on-premise and published in the cloud, there's complete flexibility in choosing development, test, and production states and where the target resides.

Release Management for Visual Studio – Workflow Automation

Maintaining Consistency in the Testing and Deployment Process

Through all stages of the application lifecycle process, it is important to maintain security and control of the state of the code, and avoid accidental deployment by managing security, and assigning and managing roles and responsibilities for releases. This is an important function of the Release Management for Visual Studio solution in identifying who has to sign off on the completion of code, who has the authority to release code, and the processes that code will follow throughout its lifecycle.

Most development teams require multiple signatures (or approvals) before code can be released to specifically prevent the accidental release of code in process. This is not to require extra paperwork or not trust individuals who are responsible for the total project, but to just put in basic checks and balances into a system, that in the era of cloud computing where things are moving very rapidly, the checks and balances are of great assistance.

Within Release Management for Visual Studios, there can be different roles for different phases of the application lifecycle so that some release approvals may require just 1 approver, whereas other releases may require several approvers. The options are flexible to ultimately meet the appropriate security, protections, and approval processes desired.

Extending Visibility to All Team Members

Lastly, within Release Management for Visual Studio is the ability to extend visibility of information to a variety of team members and stakeholders. Everything from raw collaboration information that was part of the development, bug resolution, and release process through fully customizable dashboards for single view of a variety of data points.

Logging information is centrally available for access including extraction of information from logs, reports, collaboration threads, and the like to make information on the lifecycle of the project available to those who need to know.

Part III:
Integrating Core DevOps Solutions to Microsoft Azure

10 UNDERSTANDING FUNDAMENTAL AZURE SERVICES IMPORTANT TO DEV/TEST SCENARIOS

So far in this book we've covered tools and common processes for cloud-based hosting and management, at this point we'll cover fundamental Microsoft Azure services that are leveraged by development teams specific in Dev and Test scenarios.

Using Template Gallery Configuration Images for Stock Configurations

In creating the development platform, teams need base systems to work with, whether it's a stock Windows or Linux virtual machine, a ready-made SharePoint environment, an IIS Web environment, or even an Apache Web platform environment. Microsoft Azure has dozens of pre-built templates (Microsoft and non-Microsoft) that a team could choose from. These templates can be spun up from the Azure Web Console, the templates could be spun up from a scripted (PowerShell) line command, or an automation tool like System Center could be used.

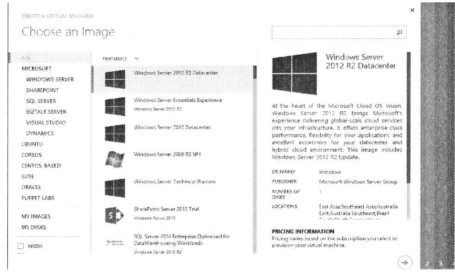

Microsoft Azure Template Gallery for Stock Templates

Regardless of the method used to create the template, the enterprise can rapidly deploy development platforms from which developers could more quickly jump right in and start writing code on the platform.

Creating or Uploading Custom Configuration Images to Use in Azure

There are cases where even the stock template that Microsoft provides may not be what the developers need, as such, Microsoft provides the ability for custom configured templates, images, and systems to be created and uploaded to Azure. These uploaded templates can be a Microsoft or non-Microsoft operating system, a Microsoft or non-Microsoft toolset, and a Microsoft or non-Microsoft configuration. There are a number of variations supported that can simply be uploaded and added to the organization's custom template library.

Once in the custom template library for the organization, systems or configurations can be rapidly spun up for the developers based on these templates.

Leveraging Rapid Provisioning for Dev/Test Projects and Scenarios

The key to deployment of templates or configurations is to do it "rapidly." While templates could be imported each and every time, it is more efficient and for development teams many times business critical to be able to spin up a configuration within minutes, rather than within hours. And the configurations might not be spun up just one at a time, but potentially dozens or hundreds of the same configuration to meet the base needs to an entire team of developers.

Rapid provisioning also might not be based off a generic template, but may be a frozen codebase that needs to be rapidly rolled out so that developers can all be working off of a specific code revision for any and all updates.

Rapid provisioning may also include the rapid rollout of an older (rolled back) version of code, something that doesn't happen too often, but when it does, something that a development team would want to be able to rollback all systems as quickly as possible so that the team would be working off the approved codebase, even if it is a step back for some reason.

Creating and Managing Build Processes

When rolling out configurations, the platform environment may need to be created and managed on demand or through some form of automation, or at times both on demand as well as with automation. The build and deployment process may just be rolled out based on an approved codebase that now all developers need to work on. Or specifically, while some teams are rolling forward with an approved codebase, another team might be rolling back to fix bugs or issues within their portion of the codebase that'll be merged or integrated with other codebase revisions down the line.

Again, it is the flexibility of the deployment process that would best help developers in the varying requirements in the development lifecycle.

UNDERSTANDING FUNDAMENTAL AZURE SERVICES IMPORTANT TO DEV/TEST SCENARIOS

11 EXTENDING CORE FABRIC INFRASTRUCTURE THROUGH AZURE NETWORKING SOLUTIONS

While the operating system platform, the Web development environment, and other development configuration customization is important in the development cycle, "fabric integration," namely core networking and like become important in the development lifecycle.

Extending On-premise Networking to Cloud Versatility

Many development teams are unaware of their options and the benefits that come with versatility of network to cloud integration. Development teams that have worked solely with internal on-premise development environments assume that connectivity to internal network resources is a given, being that they have always worked in an on-premise integrated environment. Or development teams that have been working with other cloud environments that are completely isolated from internal networking resources may just assume that's the way the cloud works, that everything is completely isolated.

However, with Microsoft Azure, the integration between on-premise resources and cloud-based platform environments is an important option for development teams. Microsoft provides Network Virtualization between traditional on-premise networks and Microsoft Azure in the cloud. In simpler terms, Microsoft allows on-premise networks to "stretch" to Azure so that virtual machines and development platforms up in Azure actually look, integrate, and behave as if they were on-premise. So

53

developers who want to do things like integrate applications to Active Directory authentication, or developers who want to integrate existing on-premise applications (databases, ERP applications, authentication tools, storage resources, etc.) don't have to do anything special with the existing applications because the existing applications will be fully accessible from the development platform provided by Microsoft Azure in the cloud.

The connectivity between on-premise networks and Microsoft Azure is a Site to Site Virtual Private Network (VPN), where either an appliance (like an edge firewall, router, or the like from Cisco, Juniper, and other hardware vendors) or simply a Microsoft Routing and Remote Access (RRAS) server can be setup to be the gateway that stretches the internal corporate network safely and securely to Microsoft Azure.

Maximizing Cloud Performance through Express Route

For enterprises that want to stretch their enterprise network to Azure and have high performance, SLA-based reliability, and better security can bypass the general Internet and connect their enterprise network to Microsoft Azure over what is called Express Route. Express Route is a dedicated connection between and enterprise to Microsoft Azure, through a point to point connection or simply integrated as an additional node off of an organization's existing MPLS network. Express Route to Azure provides a VPN-less connection, just like the enterprise might have as a connection to various sites in the enterprise over MPLS.

So instead of encapsulating all traffic over a VPN connection to Azure, the Express Route provides a faster and better managed connection. And since this connection to Azure now rides over an existing high speed connection instead of through the general Internet, the speeds, performance, security, and reliability is driven to a level that an enterprise would expect from an important and strategic connecting point.

Enabling Secured Connections through Express Route

Express Route connections also provide better security than configuring a Site to Site VPN over the general Internet. Express Route connections do not traverse the general Internet in any way, as such, beyond performance benefits, the Express Route provides a direct connection into Azure and an enterprises isolated development environment.

Whether the enterprise is using a Site to Site VPN or Express Route, since there is a connection from an internal environment to Azure resources over a private connection, the organization doesn't need to particularly expose the Azure platform to the general Internet. By default, development platforms are not exposed to the general Internet, that developers have to "open up" firewall ports of the development environment to the Internet if that is the chosen methodology.

By retaining Internal only / Internal facing connections, the organization doesn't have to worry about their application environment from being compromised from the external port. Connectivity would have to go through other centralized mechanisms to achieve the level of security desired.

Customizing Configurations to Meet the Needs of the Application

While virtual machines and application test environments can be set to internal only access and NOT opened up for external access, there are other options to isolate communications to the development platform. Microsoft Azure supports static internal addressing for virtual machines and applications, thus allowing an organization the ability to isolate the security profile for systems and environment.

Additionally, Microsoft Azure supports static internal addresses so that even the addressing of the platform environments can be directly identified and managed at any time. Just as internal on-premise services frequently have static internal addresses, now so can Azure-based applications where the same static internal addressing association is established.

Supporting Internal Load Balancing

For developers that need to have virtual scale of workloads and/or improved workload redundancy, Microsoft Azure supports internal load balancing. Rather than requiring an enterprise to setup traditional load balanced servers connected to external (or internal) load balancing appliances and tools, Microsoft can provide the load balancing as just a checkbox selection for higher availability and reliability.

Microsoft provides a variety of options for load balancing, whether it is internal, through system redundancy, through global load balancer integration, Microsoft enables enterprises to think more broadly of what all Azure can do compared to other cloud providers.

Connecting Multiple Virtual Networks

As much as Microsoft provides virtual load balancing and network virtualization, another service Microsoft provides is the ability to connect multiple virtual networks together. The process of integrating multiple virtual networks is done by establishing network traffic zones and stretching networks even across regions.

Virtual Networks may have already been established by an external management agency to help control managed resources. Supporting multiple virtual networks provides an organization the ability to leverage geo-redundancy and better manageability options.

Connecting Multiple Cloud Services to Azure Workloads

Along with the option of connecting multiple virtual networks together for redundancy, scalability, and reliability, Microsoft also provides organizations the ability of connecting multiple cloud services to Azure. A cloud service may be a storage account, may be a collection of databases, or a series of networking resources. The integration of various cloud services provides the aggregation of these various independent services to be shared, and extends the power and the capability of Azure to an extended level for organizations.

12 ENSURING SECURITY AND RELIABILITY EXPECTATIONS ARE MET WITH AZURE

When data is stored in an external datacenter such as the cloud, enterprises ask the question about security and reliability of the hosted storage location. There are various perspectives on cloud security, where cloud providers have better security than most enterprises being that the cloud hoster's business is dependent on reliability and security despite enterprises believing their internal security is better. Microsoft's security and reliability practices are shared and audited by third party firms, with reports published and made available to those interested in viewing the reported data.

Understanding Microsoft's Default Security Practices
The first place to look for information about Microsoft's default security practices for Azure is up on Microsoft's Trust Center found at: (http://azure.microsoft.com/en-us/support/trust-center/)

Microsoft's stated policy on security and reliability is that it is your data, Microsoft runs the datacenter and infrastructure that your data is stored, but does not own or manage your actual data information.

Microsoft security is multi-layer that includes:

- Facility – Physical controls, video surveillance, and clearly documented access controls
- Network Perimeter – Best practice based edge security that includes

firewalls, edge routers, intrusion detection systems, and vulnerability
scanning

- Internal Network Security – Multi-factor authentication access to
network systems, internal network layer intrusion detection, and
continuous vulnerability scanning
- Host Level Security – Continuous monitoring of all host services,
access controls, anti-malware protection, patch management,
configuration management, and systems management controls
- Application Level Security – Secure engineering protection controls,
application level anti-malware and protection, application level
monitoring and application level access controls
- Administration Security – Ongoing training, administrator auditing,
multi-level account management, and extensive screening
- Data Security – Threat and vulnerability security management,
monitoring and active response practices, data level access controls
and monitoring, file and data level integrity validation, and content
encryption

Microsoft security and reliability processes are based on industry best
practices and go through ongoing process control reviews and audit testing
to ensure that the practices keep up with the latest best practices in the
marketplace.

Understanding Microsoft's Default Privacy Policies

Microsoft's default privacy policy starts with a practice where they do
not advertise to their business customers based on content stored or
business data as part of the default services. This is a major complaint of
other cloud providers whose business models are based on advertising and
content assessment and marketing toward the data analytics of the
information stored as a service to the providers.

Microsoft's Azure infrastructure is maintained by Microsoft, however as
an enterprise, you are responsible for managing your own applications and
data, unless the specific Azure service is based on Microsoft hosting the
application and managing your data. Being that you own your data and the
management of your data, while you can pay Microsoft to geo-replicate
your data to other datacenters, it's up to you to make sure that your data
meets your enterprise backup and retention policies and practices.

Microsoft provides backup services that can be integrated as part of
your Azure services, however it is an add-on service specifically focused on
content backup, and it's up to you to determine if you want to depend on
data replication, data redundancy, and/or content backup as part of your

information management strategy.

Addressing Regulatory Compliance with Azure

For organizations that have to comply with specific regulatory requirements like the Health Insurance Portability and Accountability Act (HIPAA), Service Organization Controls (SOC) 1 or 2, European Union Model Clause, Federal Information Processing Standards (FIPS) 140-2, International Organization for Standardization (ISO) 27001/27002, Food and Drug Administration 21 CFR Part 11, and the like, Microsoft provides documented statements and 3rd party audit reports.

Owning Encryption Keys to Further Extend Security Control

For enterprises worried about the security of their information stored in Microsoft Azure, one of the things the organization can do is simply encrypt their database and/or data information as it is stored in Azure, and then keep and maintain the keys separate from Microsoft. As an example, Microsoft SQL Server provides the ability to encrypt the SQL database. So as an enterprise runs Microsoft SQL in Azure, simply encrypting the database and maintaining the encryption keys separate from Microsoft will ensure that Microsoft truly has no access to the database.

Or for content stored in Azure such as files or other data, the content can be encrypted and then stored in Azure, again providing an enterprise the ability to store and maintain data in Azure, without Microsoft having the encryption keys to access your data.

Utilizing Microsoft's Antimalware for Cloud Services and VMs

Malware continues to be a source of security breaches on systems, and Microsoft has integrated antimalware into their cloud platform to help enterprises address security in the Azure platform. With Antimalware for Cloud Services, Microsoft simplifies management and security on systems, and takes one more thing away from the tasks and responsibilities of enterprises in their management of their systems.

Enabling Geo-Replication of Data

By default, virtual machines hosted in Microsoft Azure are replicated within a datacenter so that there are at least two instances of all guest sessions within a datacenter. What an organization can choose to do is extend that intra-datacenter replication with geo-replication of the virtual machines. This geo-replication typically costs around 15% more than the base cost of running the virtual machine, but provides redundancy of systems across datacenters.

Managing Reliability through Azure SQL Database Business Continuity

Beyond just intra-datacenter replication that comes by default with all Azure virtual machine instances, and geo-replication that replicates VMs across datacenters as an added service, Microsoft also provides Azure SQL Database Business Continuity service that provides extended high availability and recoverability services. The Premium service extends restore points from 7-days in the Basic service to 35-days; provides geo-replication with Recovery Time Objective (RTO) levels under 2-hours and Recovery Point Objective (RPO) to under 30-minutes. The intent is to help enterprises gain better confidence in Microsoft's Azure cloud offerings with extended reliability and recoverability services.

13 MANAGING AZURE WORKLOADS AND SERVICES

Microsoft Azure provides a number of services that helps developers address day to day tasks more easily such as providing workload testing with cloud-based scale, enabling automation tasks from cloud-based tools, and managing workloads from Software as a Service based tools among other core functionality.

Load Testing Applications and Projects to Scale

One of the tasks that developers find themselves doing on a regular basis is spinning up workloads and conducting performance testing on the workloads to validate scalability, reliability, and working to uncover problems or bugs in application code. This process of scaling code operations has traditionally required an organization to spin up a datacenter of servers. And while server virtualization has helped developers spin up fewer physical servers through the implementation of a dozen or so virtual guest sessions for each physical server, server virtualization still requires

61

physical server deployments. Physical servers are used when workload scalability is required, however if workloads are not required, physical servers lay idle.

This is where cloud-based virtualization has greatly improved the testing scale and has driven costs down for developers as dozens, hundreds, thousands of cloud-based "systems" can be spun up to do performance and load testing, however after the testing is completed, the organization can scale back the number of cloud-based virtual machines to effectively zero, and immediately save on the cost of compute cycles and management of virtual machines.

Within Visual Studio Online, the deployment and execution of test systems can be done either on-premise or within a Visual Studio Online session, thus leveraging the cloud for test runs.

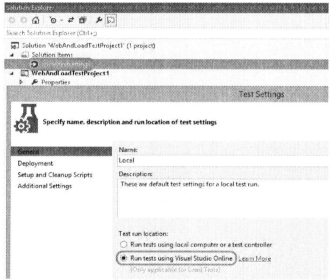

Running Workload Tests from within Azure

Utilizing Integrated Azure Runbook Automation Controls

While working with test systems in Azure, when a task needs to be run on dozens or hundreds of test machines, doing it manually one by one can take a very long time and can potentially inject errors if all systems aren't tested, or a process somehow ended up not being done identically as with other systems. System automation is key, and something that all enterprises doing application coding and testing have been developing their systems to be automated or at least have as many of the systems automated as possible.

Microsoft Azure provides Azure Automation and has a Runbook Gallery available for developers to leverage. Azure Automation is nothing more than a series of PowerShell scripts that are run as part of the sequence of operational tasks. Microsoft has developed a Runbook Gallery where developers have posted automation apps for other developers to download and use.

Azure Runbook Automation Creation

Utilizing System Center to Manage Azure Workloads and Services

Many enterprises are already using Microsoft's System Center suite of products to patch, monitor, or manage systems, and if so, System Center can be leveraged to greatly support a development environment.

System Center has components (the Configuration Manager and Virtual Machine Manager components) that'll do basic system imaging as well as ongoing patching of systems. This basic image creation and patching are the fundamentals of systems management.

However beyond the basics, System Center's components for monitoring will monitor the performance, health, consistency, and security strength of systems so that weaknesses in the system configurations can be challenged and replaced.

Beyond monitoring the health of systems, System Center Operations Manager also monitors network connections, internet connections, does application level monitoring, and monitors endpoints connections. This is particularly useful as development systems aren't always focused solely at servers, but in the age of the cloud may be a development system running as a guest session within a cloud, or purely a SaaS-based application that needs to be monitored.

When it comes to automation tasks, System Center's component for automation is the System Center Orchestrator tool. System Center

Orchestrator allows for both a graphical as well as a command line based scripted task sequences to be run. The sequence may be a process that further launches controls to review logs and systems, or it may be a full operational control that builds several new systems either on-premise or in Azure in the cloud. The possibilities for Orchestrator are virtually endless as scripted automation can take the form of almost any task that is handled by a user or administrator any time during the day.

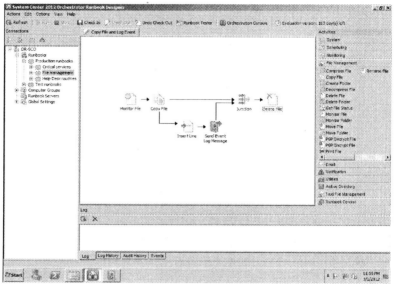

System Center Orchestrator for Runbook Automation

Utilizing Puppet and Chef to Manage Azure-based Workloads and Services

The management and automation tools leveraged in Microsoft Azure do not even need to be Microsoft-based tools, and in fact configuration management tools like Puppet and Chef are available and leveraged in Azure for managing Windows and non-Windows based guest sessions.

Chef is a configuration management tool written in Ruby and Erland and leverages a process of the creation of "recipes" that are used to configure and manage server systems. The server systems are frequently Linux-based systems, however Chef also runs on Windows and recipes are created in managing Windows-based servers as well as Linux-based servers. Common recipes include those that automatically provision and configure new systems, and also include recipes that deploy applications like MySQL, Apache, Hadoop, or the like onto a server session.

Puppet is similarly written in Ruby and provides configuration management capabilities to systems, again either running in Linux or in Windows. Puppet uses a declarative language where processes are stored in "Puppet manifests." For enterprises that leverage Puppet in their application lifecycle management process, Microsoft has a pre-configured instance of Puppet Enterprise available to be deployed as a fully operational image. This image is one of the many virtual guest session templates in the Azure Template Gallery.

Utilizing the Azure Puppet Enterprise Template

Automating Core Processes and Operational Details

Regardless of the tool used, core processes such as the deployment of a Windows or Linux operating system, the configuration of the systems IP address, services like built-in firewalls, features or services installation and enablement, installation of add-on applications, or the like can be scripted as part of the deployment and management process of the image.

Or for systems that are rapidly deployed, a script may be initiated that further customizes a base template, so a script that adds in an application or makes final changes to a configuration during the deployment or operations lifecycle.

Extending Application Management Through Visual Studios Online Application Insights

As Azure guest sessions are deployed, a development team can monitor the sessions using a tool like Microsoft System Center Operations Manager (SCOM) as previously noted, or the organization can use a cloud-based tools like Visual Studios Online Application Insights. Application Insights monitors global availability, operational performance, and usage monitoring and provides a graphical as well as a customizable table or reporting mechanism for the development team to "see" the overall health of an application, series of applications, server, or series of servers.

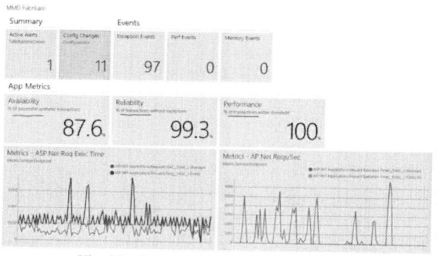

Visual Studios Online – Application Insights

A dashboard can be created that provides insight to user geography and web based usage so that performance and operational metrics can be assessed and noted by geography. This is particularly helpful if an application is working fine say for example in the United States, but users in Australia are complaining that performance is sluggish. Application Insights can break down performance by geography and note specifically the differences in performance and metrics by region.

14 UTILIZING VARIOUS TOOLS TO ENHANCE DEV/TEST SCENARIOS

The previous chapter introduced a number of tools and services available to assist developers in the creation and management of virtual guest sessions running in Microsoft Azure. In this chapter, we will extend further into other utilities, tools, and services that provide incremental support and assistance to developers in the creation, management, and ongoing operations of applications and guest sessions running in Microsoft Azure.

Maximizing the Use of PowerShell to Manage Workloads

Microsoft's scripting platform, PowerShell, provides a mechanism that can help developers built, manage, and automate processes for Windows-based virtual guest systems, but also can be used to automate the process of creating non-Microsoft based virtual machines like Linux-based systems.

PowerShell is the scripting language that is core to Microsoft's HyperV platform that is the underlying hypervisor in Azure. Since Azure allows the creation of non-Windows based guest sessions like Linux, a PowerShell script can be launched within Azure to create a Linux guest session. In fact, the Linux guest session deployment can be repeated virtually an unlimited number of times to massively build and deploy dozens, hundreds, thousands of guest sessions.

Once a Linux-based guest session is created, a datacenter operations administrator may switch to something like Puppet or Chef, initially described in the previous chapter, in the customization of the Linux guest session.

Leveraging Desired State Configuration (DSC) to Accelerate Core Tasks

When working with a development and test environment, it is extremely important that consistency is maintained across the development systems. Variations in platform code, versions of application code, and even slight variations in operational environment variables can impact the state of the coding environment.

For development teams building base operating systems, Microsoft introduced the PowerShell Desired State Configuration (DSC) in the Windows Management Framework 4.0 that provides configuration management resources when building Windows Server 2008R2, Windows Server 2012, Windows Server 2012R2, and client operating systems Windows 7 and Windows 8.1. Interestingly PowerShell DSC also provides configuration management for Linux-based systems as well.

PowerShell DSC enables the ability to install and remove server roles and features, manage registry settings on systems, configure environment variables, create directories and copy over files, and setup services and launch other system processes. The PowerShell DSC can be used to create local users and groups, install and manage applications on systems, spawn other PowerShell scripts, and then be used to discover the state of a system to confirm it matches with the desired configuration and even fix a configuration state that does not adhere to the expected standard.

```
PS C:\Users\Administrator> $params = @{
>> Namespace = 'root/Microsoft/Windows/DesiredStateConfiguration'
>> ClassName = 'MSFT_DSCLocalConfigurationManager'
>> MethodName = 'PerformRequiredConfigurationChecks'
>> Arguments = @{
>> Flags = [uint32] 1
>> }
>> }
>> Invoke-CimMethod @params
>>


                                      ReturnValue PSComputerName
                                      ----------- --------------
                                                0
```

PowerShell Desired State Configuration – Configuration Check

For organizations that have worked with Puppet and Chef, they will find PowerShell DSC to be a similar framework, one that leverages declarative language syntax that explains what the system should look like. A Management Object Format (MOF) file is created and the file is then either pushed to the node or pulled down to the node to apply the desired state.

An application, called the Local Configuration Manager, is installed by default when the Windows Management Framework is installed on the system. The LCM calls the DSC resources and performs the work of applying the required configuration settings.

Organizations that are not using a centralized management solution like Microsoft System Center Configuration Manager, or organizations that are looking for a "lighter" configuration mechanism may find the PowerShell Desired State Configuration to automate and confirm the build state without the need for external tools and systems.

Leveraging Octopus Deploy in Azure

Microsoft recently added "Octopus Deploy" support in Azure, which is an automated .NET deployment mechanism that helps developers manage the deployment of code into dev/test, or ultimately into production systems. To walk through the coding and release management process where Octopus Deploy starts to make sense, here's the lifecycle:

1) Developers create code and commit the code in the organization's existing source control system – This might be in something like Team Foundation Server, Visual Studio Online, GIT, or the like. This is up to the organization to choose.

2) Code is compiled and prepared for packaging – This might be in tools like Team Foundation Server, Visual Studio Online, TeamCity, Jenkins, or the like.

3) Application is packaged into a NuGet package for deployment – Code is then bundled together to include binaries, scripts, images, configuration files, etc and put into a NuGet package

4) Octopus takes the NuGet package and pushes it to systems – Packages are then deployed to target systems

Within the configuration there is an Octopus Deploy server along with an agent (called the Tentacle agent) that is installed on each target server. Through a Web-based dashboard, release managers queue up deployment processes. Packages are selected to be pushed to test, staging, or even production systems, ensuring that code retains consistency to each endpoint system in an environment, as properly staged through production deployments. For more information on Octopus Deploy, see http://www.octopusdeploy.com

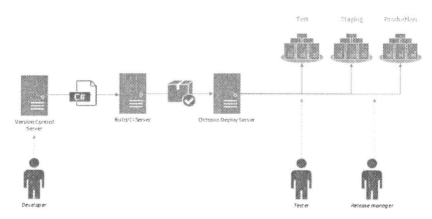

Leveraging Octopus Deploy to Manage Code Release
(graphic courtesy of http://www.octopusdeploy.com)

Utilizing Docker for Rapid Development and Deployment Scenarios

In the summer of 2014, Microsoft released the support for Docker containers for Linux in Azure. Docker is a containerized platform that allows Docker-based applications to run in an isolated, portable, and resource controlled operating environment, eliminating the dependency on base platform operating systems, hardware drivers, and system resources that typically causes variations between development platforms.

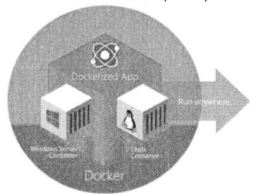

Microsoft's Docker Containers

Docker provides consistency of runtime environment between platforms, whether running in a Docker container on Windows, on Linux, on on-premise systems, on cloud-based systems, or the like. And especially as development systems shift between on-premise resources and cloud-based resources, a development team can gain confidence that their application running within a Docker container will run the same in dev, test, Windows, Linux, cloud environments, etc without the impact of external variables.

Microsoft supports Docker containers for Linux on Azure, and in Microsoft's next release of Windows in 2015, there will be built-in support for Docker containers for Windows on Azure. With the next release of Windows, Microsoft will support running .NET and other application types (node.js, Java, C++, etc) within these containers. Developers will be able to leverage the Docker ecosystem to create distributed container-based applications.

For developers already using Docker containers on Linux, Microsoft's Azure cloud platform can easily be a target hosting location for developing, testing, and running Docker-based applications. Also inherent in the integration of Microsoft's support for Docker on Azure is the support for connecting applications via the Docker Hub that allows for versatility and scalability to applications.

UTILIZING VARIOUS TOOLS TO ENHANCE DEV/TEST SCENARIOS

Part IV:
Optimizing DevOps and Application Lifecycle Management Using Business Intelligence and Azure Analytic Tools and Services

15 EXTENDING THE POWER OF DATA ANALYTICS TO APPLICATION FOCUSED INITIATIVES

For developers, the idea of capturing data to perform analytics on development processes is not always the most commonly thought of task, however development teams are now regularly tapping logs and development metrics in their day to day processes.

Testing Applications to Scale Beyond Simple Server Utilization

The shift to analytics based assessments has come about from the availability of data as well as a conscious effort by organizations to optimize application runtime characteristics. In a world where servers were purchased and capacity was based on purchased capacity, having slack in operational runtime efficiency was the norm. However in a consumption model economy where costs are directly associated with capacity, demand, and application utilization, the more efficient an application runs, the better optimized the cost is of the operation of the application.

In simplified terms, if an organization needed 100 systems, they'd buy 150 systems to just be safe in terms of having enough operational capacity, and with that much excess capacity, the development process had no incentive to make the application run more efficiently than the excess capacity provided. However in terms of cloud capacity and costs incurred based on usage, if an application is only taking up the operational demands of 50 servers, the organization can save HALF if not even Two-Thirds the cost when the organization ran 150 servers. This lower cost drops to the bottom line in terms of operating efficiencies.

This is true in terms of performance analysis. Rather than identifying that 100 servers can handle 1-million transactions, therefore if the forecast is estimated at a growth of up to 5-million transactions, in the past an enterprise might buy and host 500 servers. But what organizations have found is that scalability is not always linear. Developers have found that various components of an application may scale linearly, other components of an application may scale significantly more or significantly less.

This variation in performance based on components of an application has been the root cause of many applications "crashing" due to failure in actually testing and scaling an application based on components as opposed to a perceived aggregate. If an organization finds the search component is heavily used, it may separate the search component off the application server so that the search component can be scaled to meet the growth and demand needs of that component, while not having to scale nor impact other components of the application.

So the key has been to test each component of an application separately, segregate application runtime based on the demand forecast of each component, and then scale servers and capacity based on those demands, while optimizing the number of systems needed since in the cloud world, an organization can just as easily decrease an application farm by dozens of servers when demand decreases as it could buy and add 100's of servers to a farm to meet the growth demands of the same application.

Using Azure Logging and Information Capture Routings to Gather Data

One of the traditional methods of identifying the demand of an application is to capture logging information and server statistics to determine demand versus utilization metrics. As more users log on to an application, what impact does it have relative to memory, processor, disk storage, networking, database I/O, etc that puts stress on the environment.

If an application puts heavy stress on database transactions, adding more Web tier servers might not be of benefit as opposed to adding more capacity to the database server itself.

Enabling logging and breaking down transactional and operational stress will provide better insight to the metrics needed to assess performance and demands of an application. There are several tools that will scrape transactional data from server logs, syslogs, event logs, or the like. Microsoft has their System Center Operations Manager product that does server, application, network, database, Web, and other component level logging, tracking, and analytics. Data can even be logged with log files exported into external tools like Microsoft Excel or ported into an Azure data table or analytics stream created to track historical information.

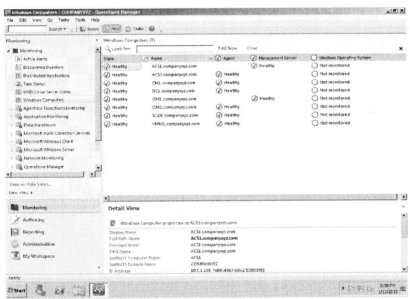

Microsoft System Center Extracting Logs for Operational Analysis

Gathering Transactional Data through Azure Analytics

One of the tools that in Microsoft Azure that helps organizations do analytics and performance modeling is Azure Machine Learning, or AzureML. AzureML is a machine learning SaaS application that takes input data and enables a data scientist to create a model to assess performance metrics for predictive analysis based on historical data.

Data can be captured, stored, and ported into AzureML like endpoint performance data, service bus data, transactional data, and the like to get varying points of perspective on an application's operational performance. By modeling the data and then projecting out overall statistics from the data into estimates in application usage growth, the development team can project the capacity, demands, operational efficiency, impact, and growth analysis of an application.

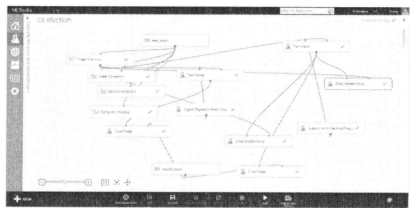

Microsoft's AzureML – Projecting Application Performance Metrics

Capturing Enduser / Customer Interactions for Better Data Analysis

As part of performance and operational analysis, many times the actual "data" being assessed isn't solely server performance or metrics coming out of log files, but may be best capturing enduser or customer interaction as a lever for doing data analysis. This frequently involves focus groups or behavior testing where an application is tested in real world usage.

Actual user interaction has significantly helped development teams understand what users experience is with an application and their interaction with the application. Testing by an internal team alone that might be somewhat familiar with the application or interface will likely navigate around the application and not run in to roadblocks and issues real world users run in to, and thus not stress an application the same way as hundreds, thousands, hundreds of thousands of real world users hitting an application for the first time.

Again, this has been the crux of many applications where everything works fine in quality assurance (QA) testing performed by professional testers, but the minute the application is released to the open marketplace, a site crashes because users unfamiliar with an application repeatedly get "stuck" in a part of an application, click a help or home button, do things

78

that stress the application in a way that was not tested in QA.

It is looking at user behaviors, dependencies, and tracking real world usage that helps organizations uncover limitations of an application, and thus allows the organization to add capacity to address stress points of the application. It is the capturing of data outside of logs and basic server utilization data plus digging into actual user interaction that has helped development teams prepare their application and services to meet the scalability requirements expected.

Analyzing Data Using Power B.I. Tools

Another set of tools that development teams have begun to leverage come in the Microsoft Power B.I. tools that help with modeling, analyzing, virtualizing, sharing, collaborating, and creating insights with data.

Power B.I. has connectors that connects SharePoint to external data sources, whether that's Excel spreadsheets, Microsoft SQL, Oracle, IBM DB2, MySQL, Sybase, PostgreSQL, Hadoop, Dynamics CRM, Microsoft Exchange, Facebook, oData feeds, Azure, and others.

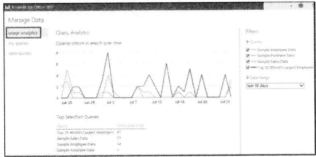

Managing Data with Power B.I.

Power B.I. provides the ability for organizations to model and analyze data where the information stored in Power B.I. can be extended for access virtually anywhere from any device.

Microsoft also provides a number of extensions to Microsoft Excel with built-in components like PowerPivot as well as there are downloadable components like Power Query and Power Map. Data can be imported into Excel, tables can be linked, models can be developed, and ultimately charts can be generated to visually analyze the data.

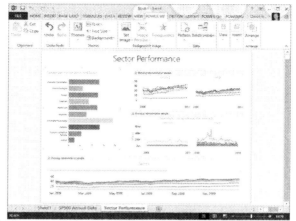

Using Power View to Display the Results of Data Analysis

ABOUT THE AUTHORS

<u>Rand Morimoto, Ph.D., MBA, CISSP, MCITP:</u> Dr Morimoto is the President of Convergent Computing (CCO), a San Francisco Bay Area based strategy and technology consulting firm. CCO helps organizations development and fine tune their technology strategies, and then provide hands-on assistance planning, preparing, implementing, and supporting the technology infrastructures. CCO works with Microsoft and other industry leading hardware and software vendors in early adopter programs, gaining insight and hands-on expertise to the technologies far before they are released to the general public. CCO has had the opportunity to work with Microsoft Office 365 in such early adopter programs allowing experts and Rand to develop tips, tricks, and best practices based on lessons learned.

<u>Guy Yardeni, MCITP, CISSP, MVP:</u> Guy is an accomplished infrastructure architect, author and overall geek for hire. Guy has been working in the IT industry for over 15 years and has extensive experience designing, implementing and supporting enterprise technology solutions. Guy is an expert at connecting business requirements to technology solutions and driving to successful completion the technical details of the effort while maintaining overall goals and vision. Guy maintains a widely read technical blog at <u>www.rdpfiles.com</u> and is a Windows MVP.